Roy White

CCEA GCSE
PHYSICS QUESTIONS

COLOURPOINT EDUCATIONAL

© Roy White and Colourpoint Creative Ltd 2021

Print ISBN: 978 1 78073 190 2
eBook ISBN: 978 1 78073 314 2

First Edition
Second Impression 2024

Layout and design: April Sky Design
Printed by: GPS Colour Graphics, Belfast

All rights reserved. No part of this publication may be reproduced, stored in a retrieval system or transmitted in any form or by any means, electronic, mechanical, photocopying, scanning, recording or otherwise, without the prior written permission of the copyright owners and publisher of this book.

Copyright has been acknowledged to the best of our ability. If there are any inadvertent errors or omissions, we shall be happy to correct them in any future editions.

The Author

Roy White taught Physics to A level for over 30 years in Belfast. He works for an examining body as Chair of Examiners for Double Award Science, Chair of Examiners for A level Life and Health Sciences, Principal Examiner for GCSE Physics and Principal Moderator for Entry Level Science. In addition to this text, he has been the author or co-author of over a dozen successful books supporting the work of science teachers in Northern Ireland.

Colourpoint Educational
An imprint of Colourpoint Creative Ltd
Colourpoint House
Jubilee Business Park
21 Jubilee Road
Newtownards
County Down
Northern Ireland
BT23 4YH

Tel: 028 9182 0505
E-mail: sales@colourpoint.co.uk
Web site: www.colourpointeducational.com

Publisher's Note: This book has been written to help students preparing for the GCSE Physics specifications from CCEA. While Colourpoint Educational and the author have taken every care in its production, we are not able to guarantee that the book is completely error-free. Additionally, while the book has been written to closely match the CCEA specification, it is the responsibility of each candidate to satisfy themselves that they have fully met the requirements of the CCEA specification prior to sitting an exam set by that body. For this reason, and because specifications change with time, we strongly advise every candidate to avail of a qualified teacher and to check the contents of the most recent specification for themselves prior to the exam. Colourpoint Creative Ltd therefore cannot be held responsible for any errors or omissions in this book or any consequences thereof.

Health and Safety: This book describes practical tasks or experiments that are either useful or required for the course. These must only be carried out in a school setting under the supervision of a qualified teacher. It is the responsibility of the school to ensure that students are provided with a safe environment in which to carry out the work. Where it is appropriate, they should consider reference to CLEAPPS.

CONTENTS

Unit 1
Motion, Force, Density and Kinetic Theory, Energy, and Atomic and Nuclear Physics

1.1	Motion	5
1.2	Force	8
1.3	Density and Kinetic Theory	10
1.4A	Energy Resources and Efficiency	13
1.4B	Work, Power, Kinetic Energy and Gravitational Potential Energy	15
1.4C	Heat Transfer by Conduction, Convection and Radiation	17
1.5A	Atoms, Nuclei and Isotopes	21
1.5B	Radioactive Decay, Dangers of Radioactivity and Half-life	22
1.5C	Uses of Radioactivity, and Fission and Fusion	25

Unit 2
Waves, Light, Electricity, Magnetism, Electromagnetism and Space Physics

2.1A	Waves	29
2.1B	Reflection, Refraction, Echoes, Sonar and Radar	31
2.1C	Electromagnetic Waves	35
2.2A	Reflection and Refraction of Light	36
2.2B	Dispersion and Lenses	38
2.3A	Electricity – Simple Circuits and Ohm's Law	41
2.3B	Electrical Resistance	44
2.3C	Electrical Energy and Power, and Electricity in the Home	46
2.4	Magnetism and Electromagnetism	49
2.5A	The Earth and Solar System, Stars and the Big Bang Model	53
2.5B	Red Shift, CMBR, Space Travel and Life on Other Planets	55

Note: This book is designed to be used by both Double Award Physics candidates and GCSE Physics candidates. Questions that should ONLY be attempted by GCSE Physics candidates are indicated with grey shading, as shown here, or otherwise indicated in the text. These questions should NOT be attempted by Double Award Physics candidates.

Note: Candidates will be in one of two tiers – Foundation Tier or Higher Tier. Questions that should ONLY be attempted by Higher Tier candidates are indicated with the words "HT ONLY" in the margin, as shown here. Foundation Tier candidates should NOT attempt these questions.

Answers: The answers for this book are available online. Visit www.colourpointeducational.com and search for *Physics Questions for CCEA GCSE*. The page for this book will contain instructions for downloading the mark scheme. If you have any difficulties please contact Colourpoint – details on the previous page.

Unit 1

Motion, Force, Density and Kinetic Theory, Energy, and Atomic and Nuclear Physics

1.1 Motion

1. A pebble takes 3.0 seconds to fall 44.1 m from the top of a cliff on to the beach below. Calculate:
   (a) the average speed of the pebble as it falls; [3]
   (b) the speed of the pebble at the instant that it strikes the beach; [3]
   (c) the rate at which the speed of the pebble was changing as it fell. [3]

2. A marble accelerates uniformly from rest down a ramp of length 2.60 m with an average velocity of 13 cm/s. Calculate: **HT ONLY**
   (a) the time taken by the marble to roll down the ramp; [3]
   (b) the velocity of the marble at the end of the ramp; [3]
   (c) the marble's acceleration, giving your answer in cm/s². [3]

3. The graph shows how the distance travelled by a pet rabbit changes over time.

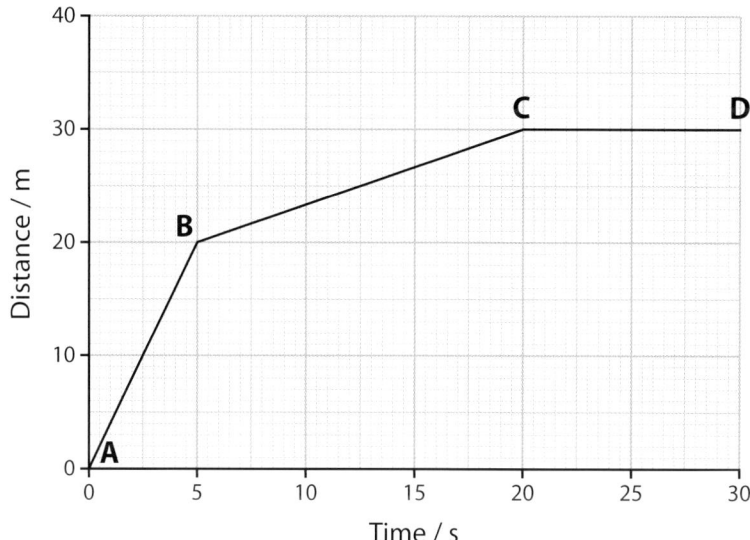

Describe the motion of the rabbit for each region (AB, BC and CD) by using one of the following phrases:

   at rest   constant speed   increasing speed

[3]

4. Below is the displacement-time graph of three dodgem cars at a fairground.

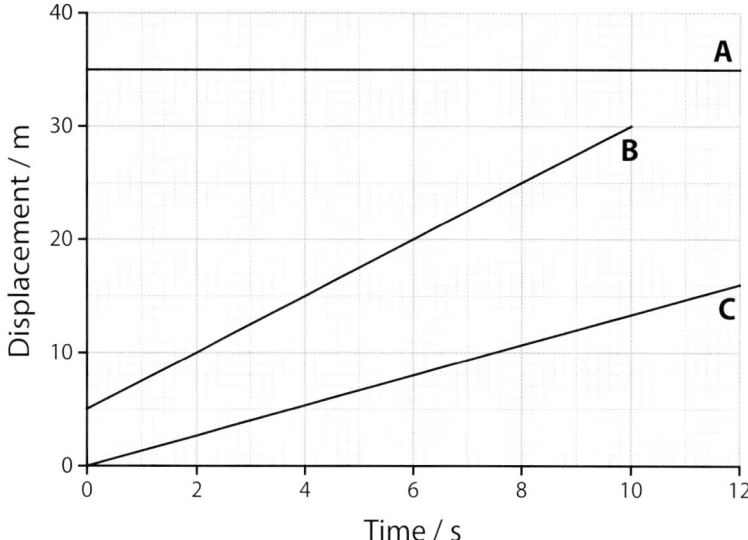

(a) Which car(s) was/were at rest at time $t = 0$? [1]
(b) Which car has a steady velocity of 2.5 m/s? [1]
(c) How far apart were cars **A** and **C** at time $t = 12$ s? [1]

5. Below is the velocity-time graph for a drone.

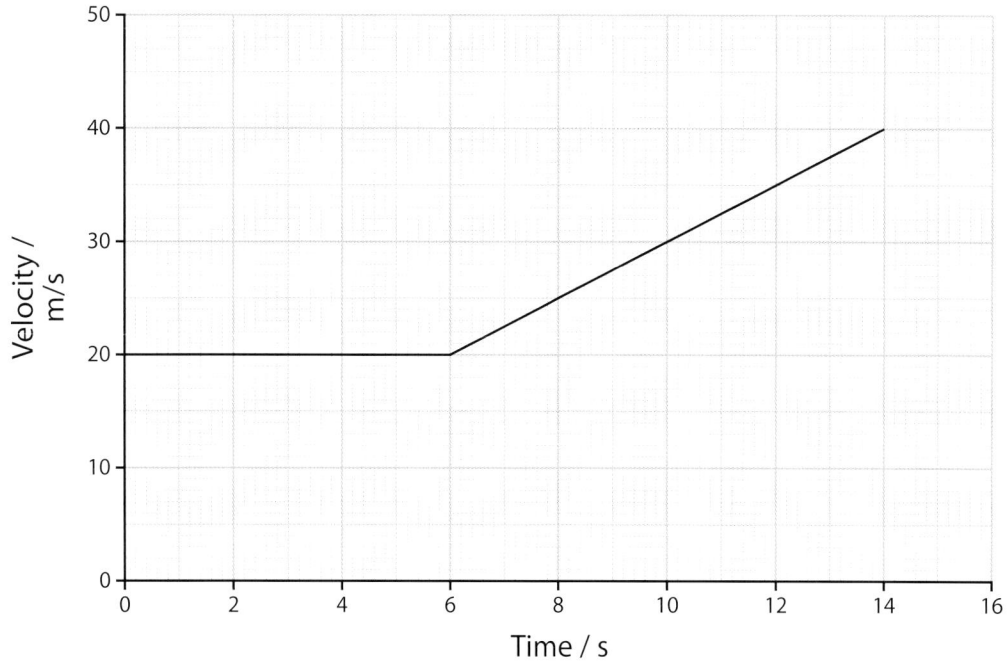

Calculate:
(a) the acceleration of the drone in the period between 6 and 14 seconds; [3]
(b) the total distance travelled by the drone in the 14 seconds of its motion; [4]
(c) the average speed of the drone in the 14 seconds of its motion, giving your answer to one decimal place. [3]

6. The graph below shows how the speed of a motor cyclist changes with time.

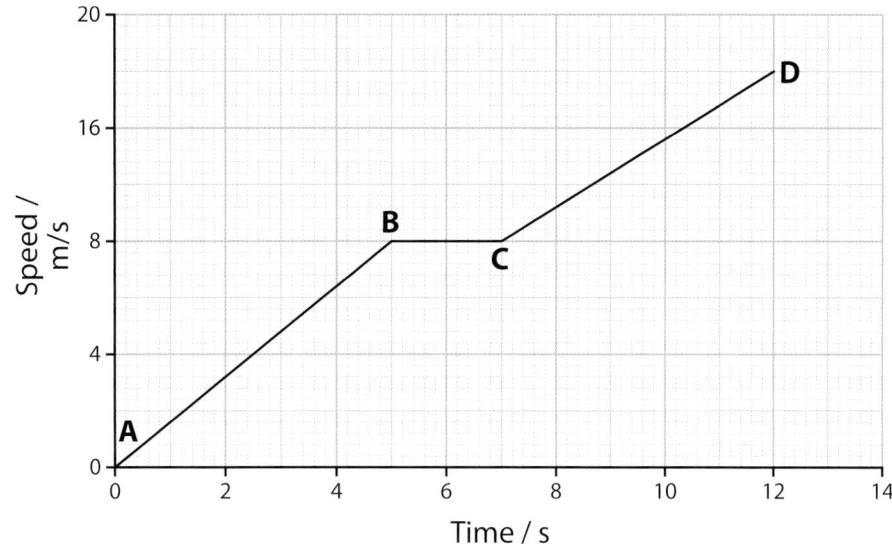

(a) In which period is the rate of change of speed least? [1]
(b) Calculate the rate of change of speed in the region **CD**. Give your answer to one decimal place. [3]
(c) How far did the motorcyclist travel in the first 5 seconds of the journey? [3]

7. A marble falls from rest at the top of a cliff and takes 2.8 seconds to reach the ground below.
(a) Write down the speed of the marble at the point when it hits the ground. [1]
(b) Calculate the average speed of the marble as it falls. [3]
(c) Calculate the height of the cliff. [3]

8. A father runs a 200 m race against his son. The boy runs down the racetrack at a steady speed. His father starts off 15 seconds after his son began to run, running down the same track at a higher constant speed. After a further 15 seconds, the father overtakes his son when they are both 120 m away from the starting line. The father finishes the race 10 seconds before his son.
(a) Calculate the speed of both the father and the son. [4]
(b) How far was the father in front of his son when he finished the race? [2]

9. A ball is thrown vertically upwards at 15 m/s. How long afterwards will it hit the ground? [4]

10. Two girls, 240 m apart, start running towards each other. One runs at 6 m/s and the other runs at 4 m/s.
(a) How long after the girls started running did they meet? [2]
(b) How much further had the faster girl run when the two of them met? [3]

1.2 Force

1. A lorry of mass 2800 kg accelerates at 2 m/s² along a motorway. If all the forces opposing motion add up to 700 N, calculate the forward force exerted by the lorry's engine. [4]

2. When a cyclist applies a forward force of 40 N on a straight, level road she moves at a steady speed. When she applies a forward force of 15 N, she decelerates at 0.5 m/s². Assuming that the force of friction has not changed, calculate the combined weight of the cyclist and her bicycle. [4]

3. One of the differences between mass and weight is that the former is measured in kg and the latter is measured in newtons. State two other differences. [2]

4. State Newton's First and Second Laws of Motion. [4]

5. A jet aircraft is flying at a constant height. Use the information shown in the diagram to calculate the aircraft's acceleration.

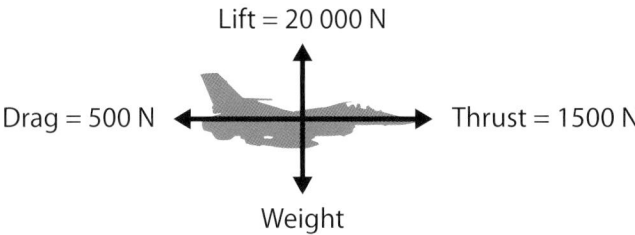

[5]

6. (a) State Hooke's Law in full. [2]
   (b) A spring is clamped vertically. When a load of 6 N is attached to the spring, its total length is 18 cm. When the applied load is 10 N, the total length is 20 cm. Calculate:
       (i) the natural (unextended) length of the spring, and [3]
       (ii) the spring constant (Hooke's Law constant). [3]
   (c) A force of 12 N is now applied to the spring used in part (b).
       What extension would you expect to observe? [1]

7. A concrete cube of side 0.8 m is used in building a bridge. When resting on the ground it exerts a pressure of 20 kPa. Calculate:
   (a) the area in contact with the ground, and [1]
   (b) the mass of the concrete cube. [4]

8. A tray overhangs a shelf, as shown in the diagram. The distance between the centre of gravity of the tray and the edge of the shelf is 15 cm. A teapot of weight 6 N rests with its centre of gravity 25 cm from the edge of the shelf.

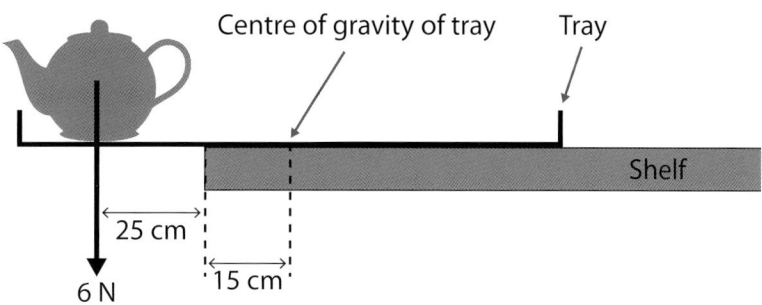

(a) Explain what is meant by **centre of gravity**. [2]
(b) State, in full, the Principle of Moments. [3]
(c) Calculate the moment of the teapot about the pivot. [4]
(d) Use your answers to parts (b) and (c) to find the weight of the tray. [3]

9. A concrete slab weighing 50 N and measuring 120 cm × 80 cm rests on the ground. Calculate the smallest force needed to raise it on one of its edges.

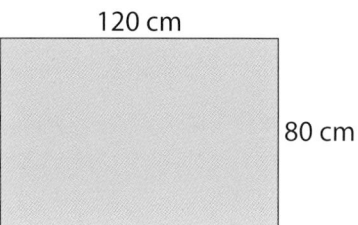

[3]

10. Describe how you would carry out an experiment using a suspended metre ruler and attached weights to verify the Principle of Moments. [6]

1.3 Density and Kinetic Theory

1. **(a)** Define what is meant by the word density. [1]
   (b) Aluminium has a density of 2.7 g/cm³. An aluminium block of mass 64.8 g is in the form of a cuboid of length 2 cm and breadth 3 cm. Find the height of the aluminium block. [5]

2. Describe how you would find the density of an unknown liquid. [6]

3. Use the results shown below to find the density of an irregularly shaped object.
   Experimental Results
   Mass of object = 60 g
   Initial volume of water in measuring cylinder = 15 cm³
   Volume in cylinder when object completely immersed = 45 cm³ [3]

4. The sketch graph drawn below (not to scale) shows how the volume of a fixed mass of **liquid** water changes as the temperature rises from about 3°C to about 100°C.

   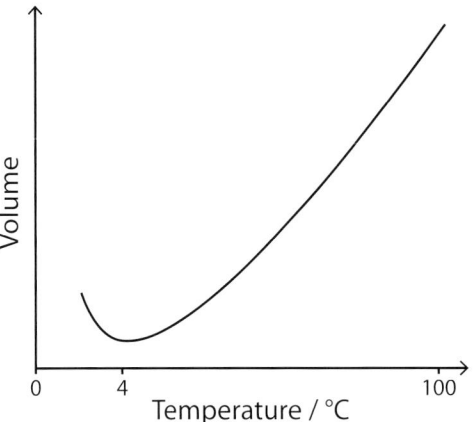

   (a) Sketch a graph to show how the density of the water changes over the same range of temperatures. [1]
   (b) Outside water pipes often burst in winter if they are not suitably lagged. Use the graph above to explain why this is so. [1]
   (c) Explain why lagging the pipes makes it less likely that the pipes will burst. [2]

5. **(a)** Describe **(i)** the motion of the molecules and **(ii)** the forces between the molecules in solids, liquids and gases. [7]
   (b) Describe and explain why the density of solids, liquids and gases are different. [5]

1.3 DENSITY AND KINETIC THEORY

6. A student places an empty measuring cylinder on a top-pan balance. He then pours different amounts of an unknown liquid into the cylinder, recording the total volume and the balance reading each time he does so.
The results are shown in the table below.

Volume of liquid / cm³	20	30	40	50	60
Balance reading / g	39	46	53	60	67

    (a) Using graph paper, plot a graph of Balance reading / g (vertical axis) against Volume of liquid / cm³ (horizontal axis), and draw the line of best fit with a ruler. [5]
    (b) Determine the gradient of the graph, give its unit and state its physical significance. [4]
    (c) State the value of the intercept on the vertical axis, give its unit and state its physical significance. [2]

7. According to legend, almost 2500 years ago, King Hiero of Syracuse asked a goldsmith to make him a crown of pure gold. After the crown had been made and paid for, rumours circulated that the goldsmith had made the crown from a mixture of gold and silver. The king asked his cousin, Archimedes, to find out if the crown was made of pure gold or not, without causing any damage to it.

Imagine you are Archimedes. You have the crown and samples of pure gold and pure silver. What would you do?

Hint: You might find it useful to look again at your answer to Question 3. [8]

8. When bridges are being built engineers regularly take samples of the concrete being used and test them to see if the concrete is suitable for the purpose. A particular project requires the concrete to have a density between 2350 and 2400 kg/m³. An engineer tests a sample of the concrete in the form of a cube of length 15 cm and finds its mass to be exactly 8000 grams. Is the concrete suitable for this project? Justify your answer. [7]

9. A technician has a large quantity of brine (salt water) of density 1.08 g/cm³. The technician is asked to prepare a sample of brine of density 1.04 g/cm³.
The technician knows that pure water has a density of 1.00 g/cm³. Calculate:
    (a) the mass of 1000 cm³ of pure water; [1]
    (b) the mass of 1000 cm³ of brine of density 1.04 g/cm³; [1]
    (c) the mass of salt in 1000 cm³ of brine of density 1.04 g/cm³. [1]

The technician measures out 500 cm³ of brine of density 1.08 g/cm³. Calculate:
    (d) the mass of salt in this 500 cm³ sample of brine of density 1.08 g/cm³. [3]
    (e) the volume of water that the technician must add to this sample to dilute it to a density of 1.04 g/cm³. *Hint: Look back at your answers to parts (c) and (d).* [2]

HT ONLY

UNIT 1: MOTION, FORCE, DENSITY AND KINETIC THEORY, ENERGY, AND ATOMIC AND NUCLEAR PHYSICS

10. The density of pure gold is 19.3 g/cm³. A jeweller mixes together 150.0 g of pure gold with 5.60 cm³ of pure copper in order to make 200.0 g of 18 carat gold from which jewellery products can be made.
    (a) Show that the volume of 150 g of pure gold is 7.77 cm³. [3]
    (b) Show that the total volume of the mixture of pure gold and copper made by the jeweller is 13.37 cm³. [2]
    (c) Use your answer to part (b) and the information given above to calculate the density of the 18 carat gold, giving your answer to 1 decimal place. [3]

1.4A Energy Resources and Efficiency

1. Which of the following are **not** forms of energy?

chemical	electrical	gravitational	potential	heat	kinetic	
light	magnetic	mass	pressure	sound	weight	[3]

2. **(a)** State the Principle of Conservation of Energy. [2]
   (b) An energy flow diagram for a car engine is shown below. Twice as much heat energy is produced as sound energy. Half of the heat energy produced is useful – it keeps the passengers warm.

   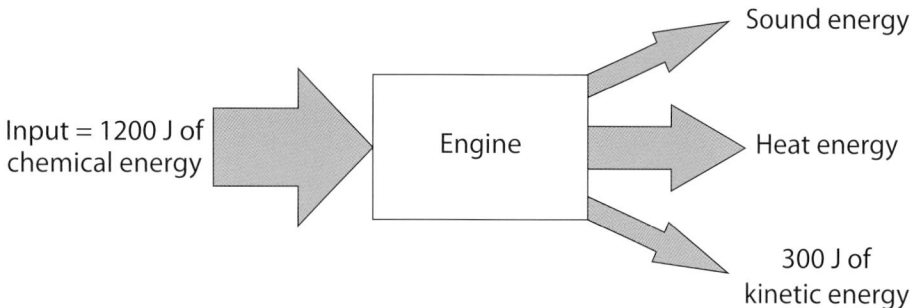

   Use the Principle of Conservation of Energy to calculate the total amount of useful energy produced by this engine. [3]

3. In which of the following scenarios is the energy used approximately equal to 1 joule?
   A A housefly walks 50 cm along a glass window pane.
   B An electron orbits a hydrogen nucleus 100 times.
   C A girl lifts an apple 1 metre off the floor.
   D A year 12 pupil runs up a flight of 12 stairs. [1]

4. **(a)** What is the difference between a renewable energy resource and a non-renewable energy resource? [2]
   (b) Name 6 renewable and 6 non-renewable energy resources. [6]
   (c) Most power stations today use fossil fuels. State two advantages and two disadvantages of using fossil fuels for this purpose. [4]
   (d) In what ways are hydroelectricity and wind energy thought to be damaging to the environment? [2]

5. State the major cause of **(a)** global warming and **(b)** acid rain. [2]

6. All the output energy from an electrical generator is measured. The results are given in the table below.

Energy form	Electrical	Heat	Sound
Energy amount / kJ	340	150	10

   Calculate the efficiency of the generator. [3]

7. A wind turbine may be used to produce electricity. The turbine blades are connected to a generator.
   (a) Copy and complete the energy flow diagram below.

   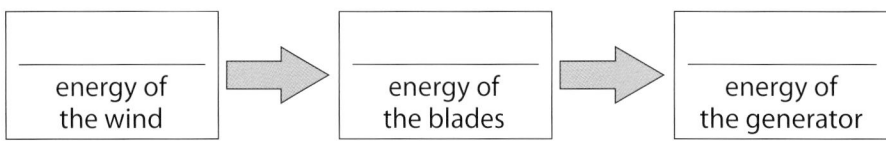

   [3]

   (b) If the generator produces 90 MJ of useful energy and has an efficiency of 30% (0.3), calculate the input energy of the wind. [3]

8. Nuclear reactors are used to produce the heat needed to generate electricity.
   (a) What nuclear process goes on in the reactor to produce heat? [1]
   (b) Name two fuels commonly used in commercial nuclear reactors. [2]
   (c) Explain why nuclear energy is considered to be non-renewable. [1]

HT ONLY

9. A ball falls from rest from a height of 10 metres to the ground below. Copy and complete the table to show its height, h, its gravitational potential energy, E_p, and its kinetic energy, E_k, at different points in its motion.

Height, h / m	10	7		
E_p / J	140		56	
E_k / J				112

[7]

10. A sledge runs from rest from the top to the bottom of a slope. Copy and complete the energy transfer diagram below to show the energy changes that take place.

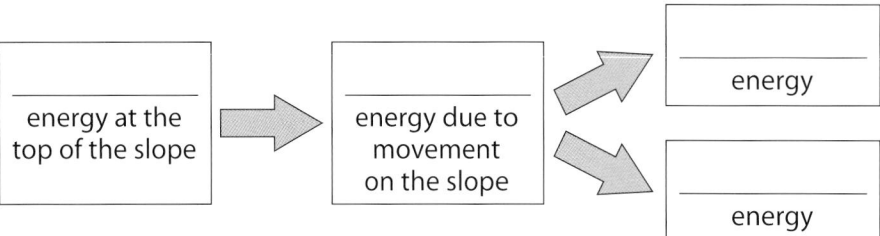

[4]

1.4B Work, Power, Kinetic Energy and Gravitational Potential Energy

1. A worker pushes a crate 2.4 m across a floor with a pushing force of 30 N.
   (a) If the crate moves at a steady speed, how much work has been done against friction? [3]
   (b) What is the significance of the fact that the crate moved at a steady speed? [2]

2. An archer shoots an arrow vertically into the air. The arrow does 60 J of work against gravity during its ascent. The maximum height reached by the arrow is 30 m.
   (a) Calculate the force of gravity on the arrow. [3]
   (b) Use your answer to part (a) to find the mass of the arrow. [3]

3. A battery stores 80 kJ of energy. If the battery is used to drive a motor which raises a 400 kg load, calculate the maximum height to which the load would rise if it was raised vertically. [3]

4. A person pushes a barrel of mass 100 kg at a steady speed up a ramp of length 200 cm. The person applies a constant pushing force of 500 N. The barrel rises vertically 70 cm when it moves 2 m along the ramp. *HT ONLY*
   (a) How much **useful** work is done by the person pushing the barrel? [3]
   (b) What is the **total** amount of work done by the person pushing the barrel? [3]
   (c) Using your answers to parts (a) and (b), calculate the work done by the person against friction. [1]
   (d) Using your answer to part (c), calculate the size of the force of friction on the barrel. [3]

5. Describe, in detail, how you could measure the personal power of a student in the laboratory. *(Note: a description given in terms of a student running up a flight of stairs is not acceptable, because it would take place outside the laboratory.)* [6]

6. (a) Explain what physicists mean when they say the output power of a motor is 5 W. [1]
   (b) How long does it take a motor with an output power of 60 W to raise a 12 kg load vertically through a height of 2.5 m? *Hint: First calculate the useful work done by the motor.* [6]

7. The output power of a small hydroelectric power station in the Sperrin Mountains is 12 kW. In a test 216 000 kg of water flow through the turbines in an hour. *HT ONLY*
   (a) Show that 60 kg water flow through the turbines every second. [3]
   (b) State the amount of electrical energy produced by the power station every second. [1]
   (c) Use your answers to parts (a) and (b) to show that the minimum average speed of the water flowing into the turbines is 20 m/s. [2]
   (d) Explain why the average speed calculated in part (c) is a **minimum** speed. [1]

8. A car is travelling along a straight, flat road with a kinetic energy of 78 400 J. An animal runs into the road in front of the car and the driver applies the brakes in order to make an emergency stop. When the car is decelerating, the average total resistive force opposing the car's motion is 5600 N.
   How far does the car travel before it comes to rest? [3]

9. A footballer strikes a ball of mass 1.5 kg sitting a rest on the ground, giving it a kinetic energy of 120 J. At a point, P, in its motion it has reached a vertical height of 5 m and lost 33 J as heat and sound due to air resistance.
   (a) Show that the ball's gravitational potential energy at point P is 75 J. [3]
   (b) Show that the ball's kinetic energy at point P is 12 J. [3]
   (c) Use your answer to part (b) to find the speed of the ball at point P. [3]

10. A squash ball of mass 150 grams strikes a wall with a speed of 20 m/s. Contact with the wall causes it to lose 36% of its kinetic energy.
    (a) Calculate the kinetic energy of the ball when it strikes the wall. [3]
    (b) Show that the ball bounces of the wall with a kinetic energy of 19.2 J. [3]
    (c) Calculate the speed with which the ball bounces off the wall. [3]

1.4C Heat Transfer by Conduction, Convection and Radiation

1. The diagram shows an experiment to compare the ability of four rods, all made of different material, to conduct heat. Drawing pins are connected to the ends of each rod with candle wax.

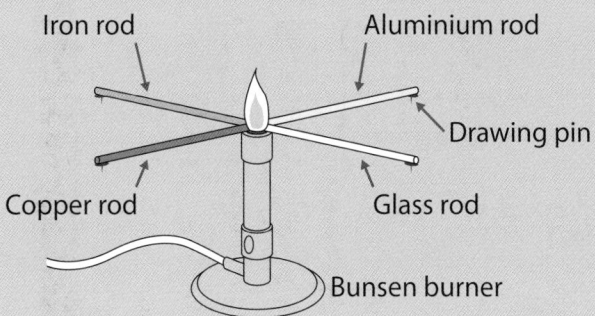

   (a) Name two properties of the rods which must be constant if the test is to be fair. [2]
   (b) Explain why the drawing pins attached to the rods eventually all fall off. [2]
   (c) State the order in which the drawing pins fall off. [1]
   (d) What conclusion can be drawn from this experiment? [2]
   (e) Use kinetic theory to explain how heat is conducted in:
      (i) metals; [6]
      (ii) glass. [5]

2. The diagram shows an experiment set up to demonstrate heat transfer in a beaker of water. The dye dissolves in the warm water and purple streamers can be seen to rise and fall.

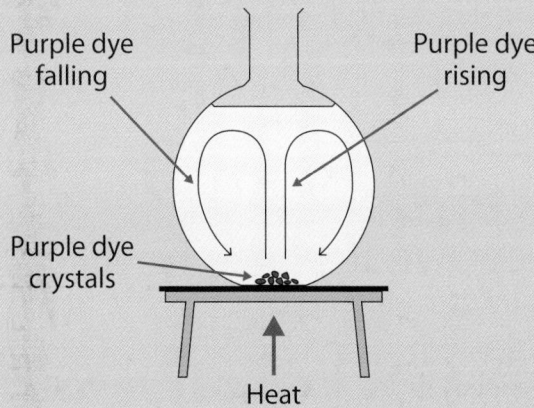

   (a) What method of heat transfer is being demonstrated? [1]
   (b) Use kinetic theory to explain what is observed. [6]

3. The diagram shows the apparatus used to compare the ability of a gloss white surface and a matt black surface to emit radiation. A thick copper plate is covered with gloss white paint on one side and matt black paint on the other. The copper plate is heated with a Bunsen burner until it is very hot. A hand is then held about 30 cm from each side in turn.

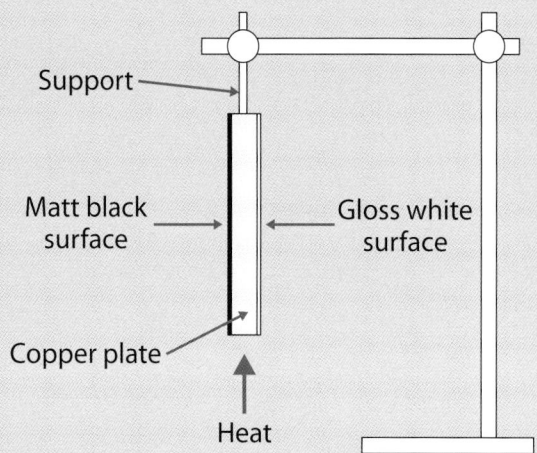

(a) Why is copper used in this experiment? [3]
(b) What does the person carrying out this experiment experience when their hand is held 30 cm from each side in turn? [1]
(c) What explanation is generally given to explain this observation? [1]

4. Two aluminium plates are suspended the same distance from the flame of a Bunsen burner. Identical corks are attached to each plate using candle wax.

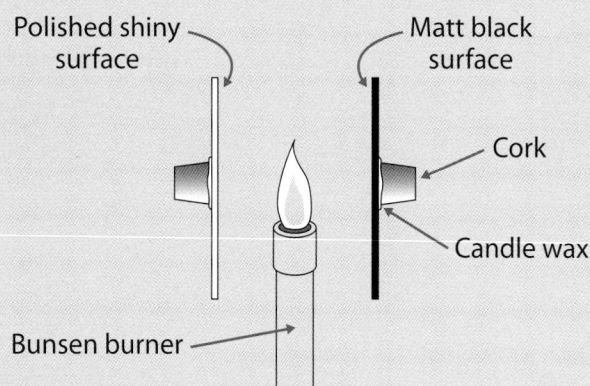

(a) From which plate does the cork fall first? [1]
(b) What explanation is generally given to explain this observation? [1]
(c) What does the experiment demonstrate about the ability of the surfaces to reflect radiation? [1]

5. The apparatus shown below is sometimes used to demonstrate heat transfer in air. The smoke from the smoking straw moves down chimney **B**, moves towards the candle flame and then moves up chimney **A**.

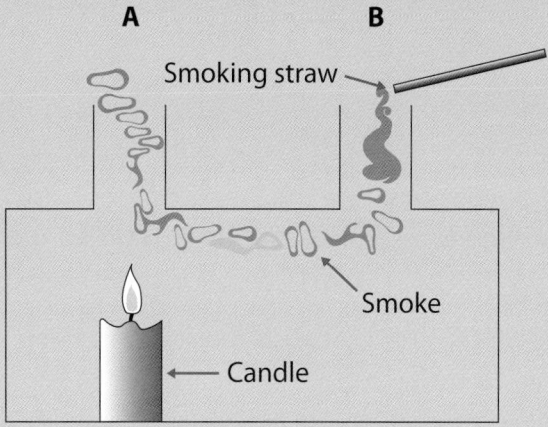

(a) What method of heat transfer does this apparatus demonstrate? [1]

(b) The smoke from a straw generally rises. Why does the smoke from this straw move down chimney **B**? [1]

(c) Explain the movement of smoke through the apparatus in terms of kinetic theory. [5]

6. A garden gate is made of metal. On a very cold winter day a student touches the gate with their hand and says:

"The metal is very cold when I touch it. That is because the gate has transferred its low temperature to my hand."

The student's explanation is wrong. What is the correct explanation as to why the metal gate is cold to touch? [3]

7. Copy and complete the table below by filling in the blanks to show the main ways by which heat loss from a person's home can be minimised. [10]

Heat loss through	Method of reducing heat loss	How losses are reduced
Walls	_____	The cavity between the outside and inside walls is filled with _____.
Roof	_____	_____ or _____ wool or polystyrene beads are placed between the joists and rafters to reduce heat loss through the roof by _____ and _____.
Windows	_____	The two glass panes trap _____. A trapped gas is a much better _____ than the glass used. So the heat lost by conduction is greatly reduced.

19

8. The diagram shows a vacuum (or Thermos) flask designed to keep liquids at a constant temperature.

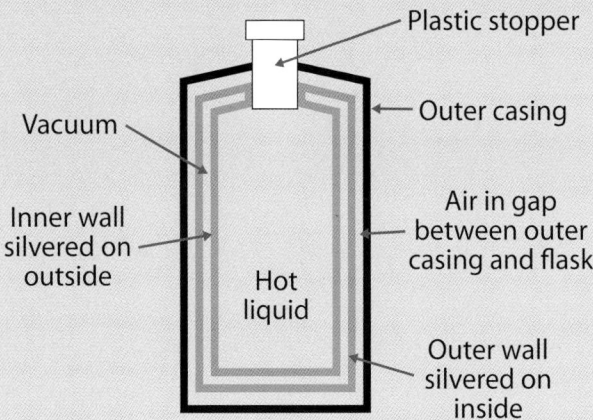

Explain how the design of the flask reduces heat loss by:
(a) conduction and convection; [1]
(b) radiation. [4]

1.5A Atoms, Nuclei and Isotopes

1. (a) What were the main features of Thomson's "Plum Pudding" model of the atom? [2]
   (b) Name the two physicists who gave their names to the modern theory of atomic structure. [2]
   (c) In what ways is the modern theory different from Thomson's theory? [4]

2. Describe, in outline, the Rutherford alpha-particle scattering experiment and its principal observations and deductions. [6] **HT ONLY**

3. (a) Explain why atoms are electrically neutral. [2]
   (b) Copy and complete the table below to show the relative masses, charges and locations of the particles that make up an atom.

Particle	Relative mass	Relative charge	Location
		0	
			Orbits the nucleus
		+1	

   [3]

4. A nucleus is designated by the symbol $^A_Z X$.
   (a) What names are given to the numbers A and Z? [2]
   (b) What information is given by the symbol X? [1]

   A certain nucleus has the symbol $^{235}_{92}U$.
   (c) How many protons, neutrons and electrons are in the nucleus of this atom? [3]

5. (a) Describe what physicists mean by the word **isotopes** in terms of the particles which are found in the nucleus. [2]
   (b) Which two of the following are isotopes?

   $^{12}_6 A$ $^{13}_6 B$ $^{12}_7 C$ $^{11}_8 D$

   (Note the letters A, B, C and D are used for identification purposes; they are not the symbols of elements.) [1]

1.5B Radioactive Decay, Dangers of Radioactivity and Half-life

1. (a) What is radioactivity and where does it come from? [2]
   (b) Copy and complete the table below to show the properties of alpha, beta and gamma radiation.

Radiation	Relative mass*	Relative charge*	Nature	Range in air	Stopped by	Ionising effect
Alpha	4					
Beta					Few mm aluminium	
Gamma			High energy electromagnetic wave	Unlimited		Very weak

*Compared to the proton
[11]

   (c) Radioactivity is both random and spontaneous. What does this mean? [2]

2. Copy and complete the following nuclear decay equations by writing the appropriate numbers or symbols in the boxes.

   (a) $^{235}_{\square}U \rightarrow ^{\square}_{90}Th + ^{\square}_{2}\square$ [4]

   (b) $^{\square}_{\square}C \rightarrow ^{14}_{7}N + ^{\square}_{\square}\beta$ [4]

   (c) $^{\square}_{\square}Ra \rightarrow ^{228}_{88}\square + \gamma$ [3]

3. (a) What is background radiation? [1]
   (b) State 3 sources of background radiation. [3]
   (c) How is background radiation taken into account when doing experiments with radioactive sources? [2]

4. Describe how you would measure the range of alpha particles in air. [6]

5. Copy and complete the following statements about the relative dangers linked with radiation from radioactive sources, by filling in the blanks.

- Alpha radiation is not as dangerous if the radioactive source is outside the body, because it cannot pass through the _____ and is unlikely to reach _____ inside the body.

- Beta and gamma radiation can _____ the skin and cause _____ to cells.

- Alpha radiation will damage cells if the radioactive source has been _____ or _____.

- All three forms of radiation can cause _____. [7]

6. Describe four steps that should be taken when handling radioactive sources to minimise the risk to those using them. [4]

7. (a) What is meant by the term "half-life" in radioactive decay? [2]
(b) The activity of a radioactive material falls from 1000 counts/second to 125 counts/second in 21.6 hours. Find its half-life. [3]
(c) The graph shows how the activity of a radioisotope changes with time. Estimate the half-life of the source.

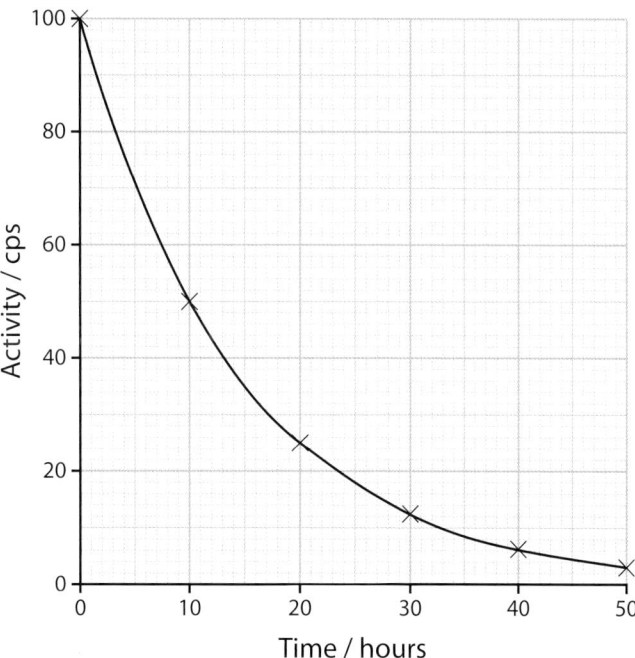

[1]

8. The activity of a radioactive source is measured every 10 minutes. The results are shown in the table.

Activity / counts per second	1500	900	540	324	194	117
Time /minutes	0	10	20	30	40	50

   (a) Plot a graph of activity (vertical axis) against time (horizontal axis) and draw a smooth curve through the data points. [5]
   (b) Use the graph to find the activity after 25 minutes. [1]
   (c) After what time is the activity equal to 1000 cps (counts per second)? [1]
   (d) Estimate the half-life of this source. [1]

9. Polonium-210 has a half-life of 138 days.
   The current activity of a sample of polonium-210 is 32 cps.
   How long will it take the activity of this sample to fall to 1 cps? [3]

10. A radioactive isotope has a half-life of 5 hours. It arrives in a hospital with an activity of 60 cps. The time taken between the removal of the isotope from a nuclear reactor and its arrival in the hospital is 20 hours. What was its activity when it was removed from the reactor? [2]

1.5C Uses of Radioactivity, and Fission and Fusion

1. State one use of radioactivity in each of the following:
   (a) industry, [1]
   (b) medicine, [1]
   (c) agriculture. [1]

2. The diagram shows the apparatus used in the manufacture of paper from pulp.

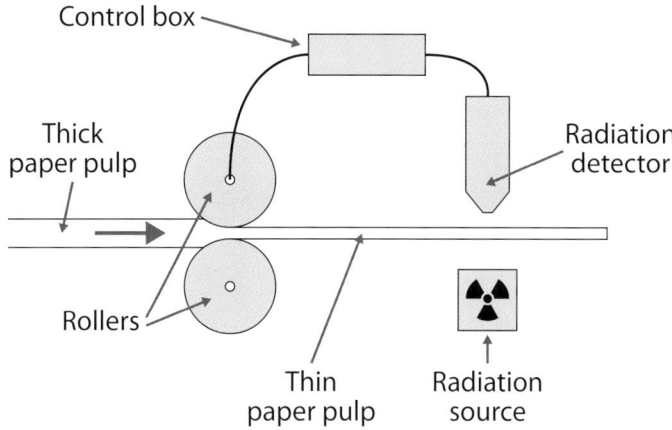

   (a) Which type of emitter, alpha, beta or gamma, should the radioactive source be?
       Explain the reason(s) for your answer. [3]
   (b) Should the manufacturer use a radiation source with a long or a short half-life?
       Explain the reason(s) for your answer. [2]
   (c) Explain how the system determines whether the rollers need to be adjusted to
       maintain a constant thickness for the paper pulp. [5]

3. The diagram shows a smoke detector. The air gap between the source and the detector is about 1 cm wide.

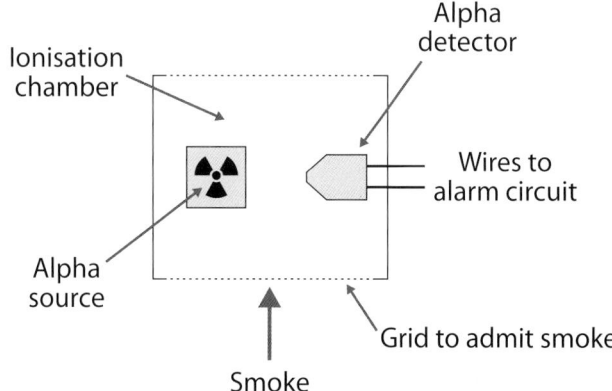

   When there is no smoke, ionisation occurs in the air between the source and the detector.
   (a) Explain what is meant by ionisation. [2]

Provided enough ions arrive at the alpha detector, no current is passed to the alarm circuit and the alarm is silent.

(b) Explain how smoke coming between the alpha source and the detector causes the alarm to ring. [2]

(c) Explain why a radioactive source of beta particles or gamma radiation would not work in this type of detector. [1]

A manufacturer can choose americium-241, which has a half-life of approximately 460 years, or neptunium-235 which has a half-life of about 435 days. Both are sources of alpha-particles.

(d) Which isotope is the better choice for a smoke detector? Give a reason for your answer. [2]

4. Carbon in the human body consists of two isotopes, $^{12}_{6}C$ and $^{14}_{6}C$. Every gram of carbon from a living person has a count rate of 16 counts / minute due to the radioactivity of $^{14}_{6}C$. This count rate remains the same throughout a person's life, but starts to decrease on the death of the person. The half-life of $^{14}_{6}C$ is 5600 years. The other isotope is not radioactive. Archaeologists can use carbon dating to find out how long ago human bodies died.

A long-dead body of a human is removed from a bog in Southern Europe. A sample of carbon of mass 14 grams, removed from the body, had a radioactivity of 56 counts per minute.

(a) The count rate from living bodies is constant because the $^{14}_{6}C$ is constantly being replaced. How? [1]

(b) Calculate the activity of 1 gram of the carbon in the body of this person. [1]

(c) Use your answer to part (b) and the half-life of to estimate how many years ago the person died. [2]

5. The nucleus of the element uranium is represented by the symbol $^{235}_{92}U$.

(a) (i) What is the mass number of uranium? [1]
(ii) How many neutrons does the uranium nucleus contain? [1]
(iii) What is the total number of particles in the uranium nucleus? [1]

(b) Uranium $^{235}_{92}U$ is formed when an unstable nucleus of plutonium (Pu) decays and emits an alpha particle. Copy and complete the nuclear equation below which describes this reaction:

$$\boxed{}Pu \rightarrow \,^{235}_{92}U + \boxed{}\alpha$$

[4]

6. **(a)** What is nuclear fission? [4]

(b) Fission reactors provide about 18% of the UK's electricity needs and this is expected to rise to over 30% by 2035. Give an account of what happens in a nuclear reactor. In your description you must:
- identify the isotope uses as the fuel;
- identify the particle which initiate fission;
- state what happens in the fission reactor;
- state one of the hazards associated with nuclear fission. [6]

1.5C USES OF RADIOACTIVITY, AND FISSION AND FUSION

7. (a) What is nuclear fusion? [2]
  (b) Where does nuclear fusion occur naturally? [1]
  (c) There are some major technological problems associated with building and running a fusion reactor. State two of them. [2]
  (d) (i) Copy and complete the equation below which describes a nuclear fusion reaction.

$$^{2}_{1}H + ^{3}_{1}H \rightarrow ^{\square}_{\square}He + ^{1}_{0}n$$

[2]
  (ii) Identify the particle $^{1}_{0}n$. [1]

8. (a) State one advantage and one disadvantage to a local community of having a nuclear fission reactor nearby. [2]
  (b) Although nuclear fission itself does not release carbon dioxide, some argue that the nuclear industry does cause the release of significant amounts of greenhouse gases into the atmosphere. Explain why. [1]
  (c) Two names which are sometimes heard in the nuclear debate are Chernobyl and Fukushima. Why are these names relevant to the debate? [4]

9. (a) It is sometimes said that the fuel resources for nuclear fusion fuel rare almost inexhaustible. Where would these resources come from? [2]
  (b) How much more energy per kilogram of fuel does fusion release when compared with burning coal? [1]
  (c) State two major environmental advantages of fusion when compared with fission and fossil fuels. [2]

10. (a) What do the letters ITER stand for in the context of nuclear fusion? [1]
  (b) Briefly describe the ITER project and explain why it is necessary. [2]

Unit 2
Waves, Light, Electricity, Magnetism, Electromagnetism and Space Physics

2.1A Waves

1. State the difference between longitudinal and transverse waves in terms of the vibrations of the particles. [4]

2. Give two examples of:
   (a) transverse waves, [1]
   (b) longitudinal waves. [1]

3. As applied to a longitudinal wave, define the terms:
   (a) frequency, [1]
   (b) wavelength, and [1]
   (c) amplitude. [2]

4. A boy throws a stone into a pond and observes the waves as they move towards him. The graph below shows how the displacement of the water at a particular point changes with time.

   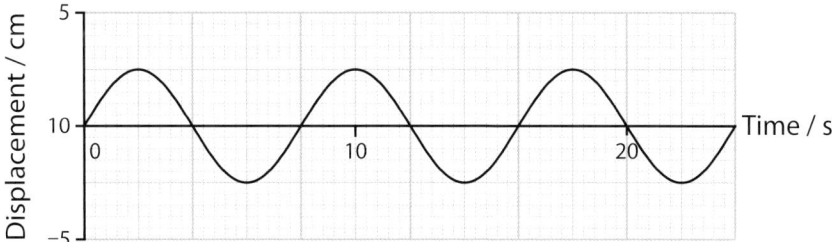

   (a) State the amplitude of these waves. [1]
   (b) Use the graph to find the frequency of the waves. [2]
   (c) Explain why it is not possible to find the wavelength of these waves from the graph. [1]

5. All waves transmit energy. What evidence can you give that sound waves transmit energy? [1]

6. The vertical distance between the crest and trough of the waves in a wavetrain is 30 cm. The horizontal distance between the first peak and the sixth peak is 45 cm. The speed of these waves is 36 cm/s. Calculate:
   (a) the amplitude of the waves, [1]
   (b) the wavelength of the waves, [2]
   (c) the frequency of the waves, [3]
   (d) the number of these waves which would pass a stationary observer every minute. [2]

UNIT 2: WAVES, LIGHT, ELECTRICITY, MAGNETISM, ELECTROMAGNETISM AND SPACE PHYSICS

7. Copy and complete the table below by filling in the blank lines. Take care with the units. The first row is already complete, as an example.

Wavelength	Frequency	Speed
2 m	5 Hz	10 m/s
12 cm	500 Hz	_____ m/s
18 mm	_____ Hz	2.7 m/s
_____ mm	5 kHz	8 m/s
5×10^{-7} m	_____ Hz	3×10^8 m/s

[4]

8. Three students observe waves travelling along a slinky spring. One student says:

    "The time between the first compression passing a fixed point and the tenth compression passing the same fixed point was 4.5 seconds."

    The second student says:

    "And I measured the distance between the first and the tenth compression. It was 90 cm."

    The third student says:

    "That would make the speed of the waves 0.45 times 9 which makes 4.05 cm/s."

    Their teacher commented:

    "If your observations are right, the speed of the waves was 20 cm/s."

    Explain where the third student made their mistakes. [2]

9. There is an analogy between the behaviour of water waves passing from shallow water into deep water and the behaviour of light waves when they refract.
    (a) What is an analogy? [1]
    (b) What, for light waves, is analogous to the shallow water and the deep water? [1]
    (c) What is observed to happen to the wavelength of water waves as they pass from shallow water into deep water? [1]
    (d) What happens to the wavelength of light waves when they pass from glass into air? [1]

10. (a) What is the range of frequency of audible sound? [2]
    (b) What name is given to sound above the upper frequency limit? [1]
    (c) Give one application of the type of sound you stated in part (b) in:
        (i) medicine, [1]
        (ii) industry. [1]

2.1B Reflection, Refraction, Echoes, Sonar and Radar

1. The diagram shows three wavefronts in water travelling towards a barrier. The wavefronts are reflected from the barrier. Copy the diagram and on it draw:
   (a) an arrow representing the reflected ray, starting at point **P**; [1]
   (b) three reflected wavefronts, taking care about their direction and wavelength. [3]

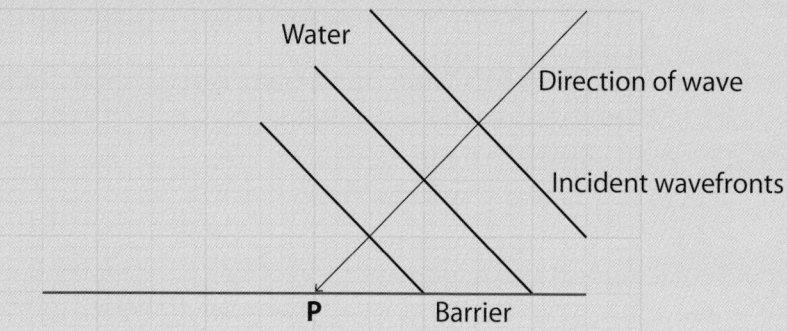

2. The diagram shows three wavefronts travelling in deep water towards a boundary with shallow water. The wavefronts are refracted as they enter the shallow water. Copy the diagram and on it draw:
   (a) an arrow representing the refracted ray, starting at point **P**, [1]
   (b) three refracted wavefronts, taking care about their orientation and wavelength. [3]

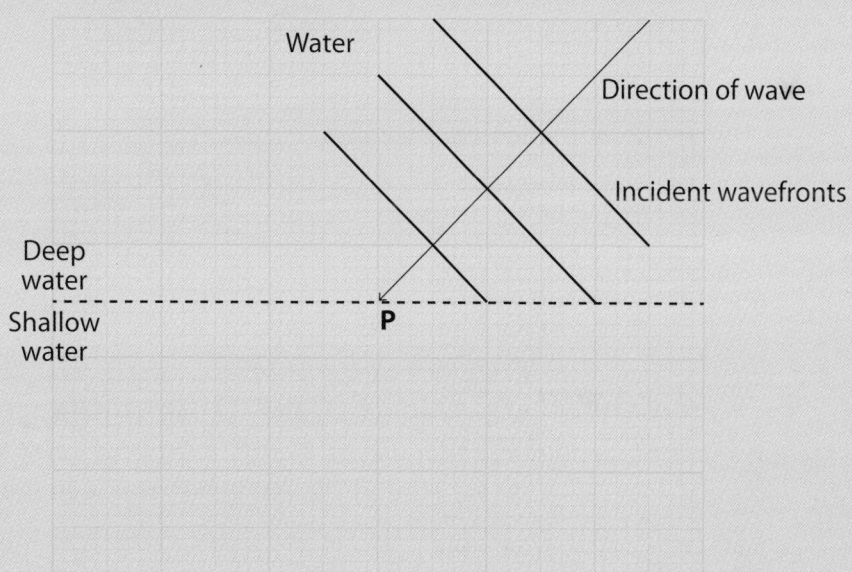

3. Certain water waves in deep water have a wavelength of 1.8 cm and a speed of 4.5 cm/s. When they refract into shallow water they travel at 3 cm/s.
   Find the frequency of these waves in shallow water. [4]

4. **(a)** What is an echo? [1]
(b) Tom and Pádraig are on a flat beach facing a tall, vertical cliff, as shown in the diagram.

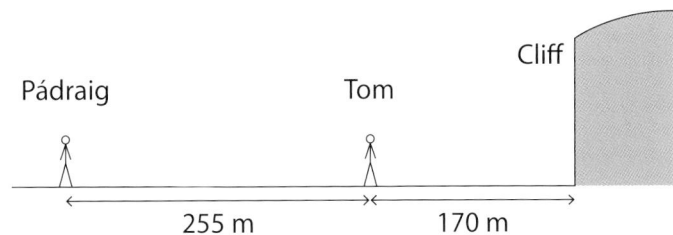

Tom is 170 m from the cliff and 255 m from Pádraig. Pádraig calls out to Tom.
Tom hears Pádraig's shout twice. The second time is exactly one second after the first.
  (i) Explain how this could have happened. [2]
  (ii) Use the data to calculate the speed of sound in air. [2]

5. A fishing trawler sends out a pulse of ultrasound. Exactly 0.3 s after sending out the ultrasound, an echo from a shoal of fish is picked up by the trawler. The speed of ultrasound in seawater is 1500 m/s.

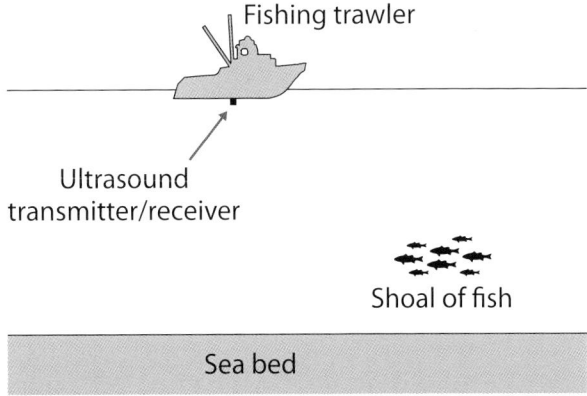

(a) Calculate the distance between the fish and the ultrasound transmitter. [4]

A short time after receiving the first echo, a second echo is detected.
(b) Explain the origin of the second echo. [1]

6. **(a)** What is the difference between radar and sonar? [2]
(b) Explain why radar, rather than sonar, is used to detect aircraft in flight. [2]
(c) A radar station sends out a pulse of radar waves. Exactly 1.5 milliseconds later, the echo from an aircraft is received at the station. If radar waves travel at 300 000 km/s, how far was the aircraft from the radar station? [4]

7. Ultrasound is used to check on the development of a baby in the womb by measuring the width of the child's head, as shown in the diagram.

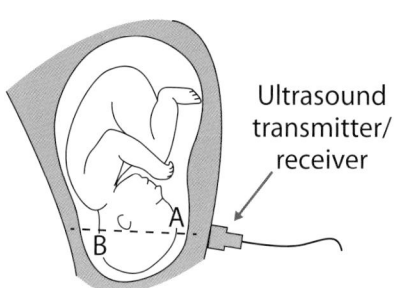
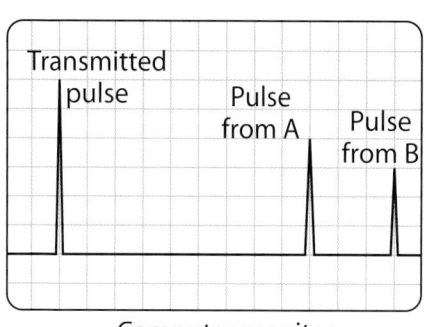

When ultrasound reaches the baby's head at A, some ultrasound is reflected back to the detector and produces pulse A on the computer monitor. Some ultrasound travels through the baby's head to point B. The reflection from B produces pulse B on the computer monitor. Each horizontal division on the monitor corresponds to a time of 50 microseconds.

(a) By counting squares, calculate the time interval between the arrival of pulse A and the arrival of pulse B at the detector. Give your answer in microseconds. Remember that 1 microsecond is 0.000 001 s. [1]

The speed of ultrasound in the baby's head is 1500 m/s.

(b) Use your answer to part (a) to show that the width of the baby's head is just over 110 mm. [4]

(c) Suggest a reason why the height of pulse B is slightly less than that of pulse A. [1]

8. The lines in the diagram below are the crests of straight water ripples moving to the right.

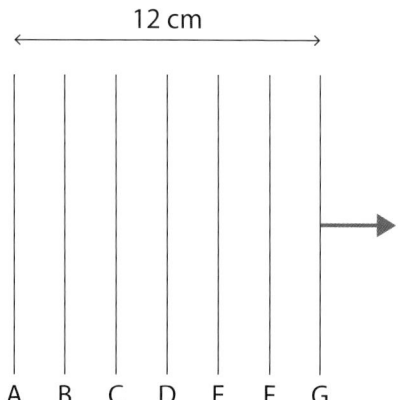

(a) Calculate the wavelength of the ripples. [2]

It takes 20 seconds for ripple A to move to the position now occupied by ripple F.

(b) Calculate the frequency of the ripples and their speed. [5]

UNIT 2: WAVES, LIGHT, ELECTRICITY, MAGNETISM, ELECTROMAGNETISM AND SPACE PHYSICS

9. Ultrasound travels at 6000 m/s in a steel railway track. An ultrasound source emits a pulse which reflects from a crack below the surface. If the echo is detected by the ultrasound receiver 20 microseconds after the pulse was emitted, calculate how far the crack is below the surface.
    Remember that 1 microsecond is 0.000 001 s.

    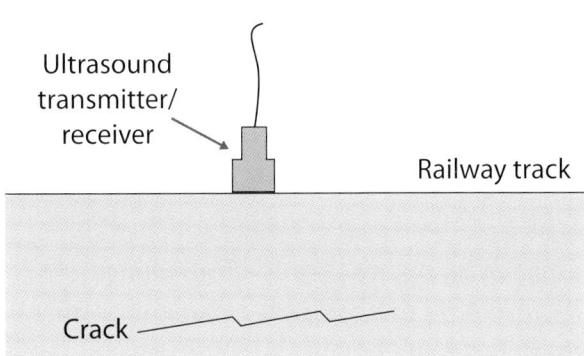

    [4]

10. Ultrasound is used in medicine to accelerate the healing of bone fractures. A particular ultrasound wave has a frequency of 1.5 MHz and a wavelength of 1000 micrometres travels through bone. A different pulse of ultrasound has a frequency of 2.0 MHz. Assuming that the two pulses travel at the same speed in bone, calculate the wavelength of the second ultrasound pulse.
    Remember that 1 microsecond is 0.000 001 s and that 1 MHz is 1 000 000 Hz. [7]

2.1C Electromagnetic Waves

1. State one property which is unique to all electromagnetic waves. [1]

2. List the members of the electromagnetic wave family in order of increasing frequency. [2]

3. The distance from a radio transmitter to an airport is approximately 900 km. A radio signal of wavelength 1500 m and frequency 200 kHz is transmitted from the radio transmitter. How long after transmission does it arrive in the airport? [4]

4. Prolonged exposure to ultraviolet light can cause skin cancer. State two ways in which a person can reduce their risk of skin cancer due to ultraviolet light. [2]

5. Infrared light is used in TV remote controls. In what way can infrared light cause harm? [1]

6. Three members of the electromagnetic wave family are: microwaves, ultraviolet light and X-rays. This list is in no particular order. Copy and complete the table below by entering the names of the four other members of the electromagnetic family of waves in the correct boxes.

Name of wave	Typical wavelength / m
	1×10^{-5}
	1000
	1×10^{-11}
	5×10^{-7}

[4] HT ONLY

7. Give two reasons why gamma rays are much more likely to cause cancer of organs such as the liver, than ultraviolet light. [2]

2.2A Reflection and Refraction of Light

1. State the Law of Reflection of Light. [1]

2. Copy the diagram below and label the normal, the incident ray, the reflected ray, the angle of incidence and the angle of reflection. [5]

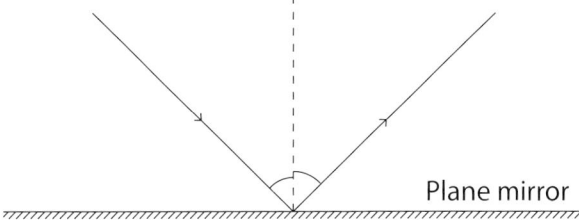

3. State five properties of the image in a plane mirror. [5]

4. Two mirrors are inclined at 90° to each other. A ray of light is incident on the first mirror, M_1, with an angle of incidence of 40°. The reflected ray then falls incident on the second mirror, M_2, as shown in the diagram below.

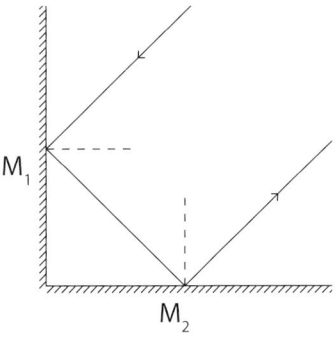

   (a) Calculate the angle of reflection at the second mirror. [5]
   (b) Comment on the directions of the incident ray on M_1 and the reflected ray from M_2. [1]

5. A horizontal light ray strikes a mirror inclined at an angle x to the horizontal. The reflected ray is directed at a 60° angle **to the horizontal.** Calculate the size of the angle, x, that the mirror makes with the **horizontal ground**.

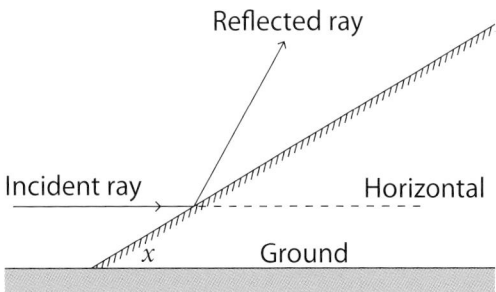

[2]

6. (a) What is refraction in the context of a ray of light? [1]
   (b) Draw a diagram to show the refraction of light as it passes from glass to air. [2]
   (c) It is possible for light to pass from a rectangular glass block into the air without being refracted. Draw a ray diagram to illustrate how this would occur. [2]

7. What happens to the wavelength, frequency and speed of light when it passes from air into glass? [3]

8. Copy ray diagrams A and B below.

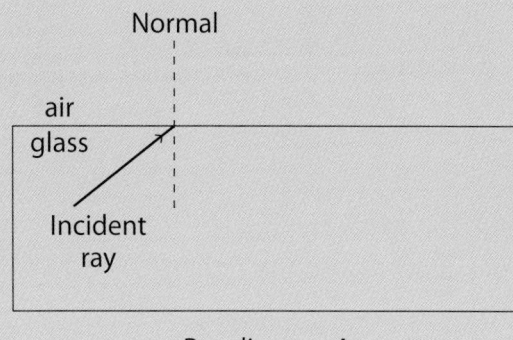

Ray diagram A   Ray diagram B

   (a) On your copy of diagram A, show what happens when the ray of light in the rectangular block of glass is incident on the glass-air boundary and the angle of incidence is equal to the critical angle. [2]
   (b) On your copy of diagram B, show what happens when the angle of incidence is greater than the critical angle. [2]

9. Describe how you could measure the critical angle of glass using a semi-circular glass block. Include ray diagrams to illustrate your description of the experiment. [9]

10. (a) What are optical fibres and how do they work? [5]
    (b) Give one medical and one non-medical use of optical fibres. [2]

2.2B Dispersion and Lenses

1. When light enters a glass prism it is dispersed, as shown in the diagram below, into its constituent colours.

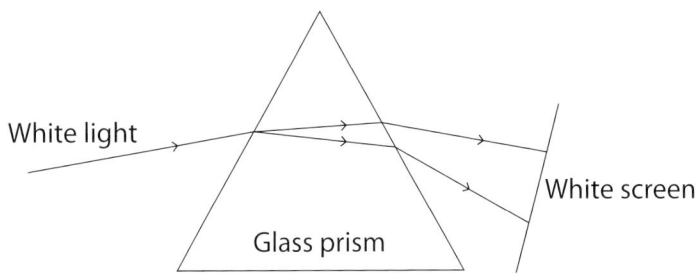

    (a) Why does dispersion take place? [1]
    (b) Name the colours, in order, that can be seen on the white screen. [1]
    (c) What name is given to the collection of colours observed on the screen? [1]
    (d) State which colour is refracted most. [1]
    (e) Explain why this colour is refracted the most. [1]
    (f) Which colour travels fastest in glass? [1]
    (g) Use the analogy with the refraction of water waves to suggest what happens to the wavelength and frequency of light waves when they pass from air into glass. [2]

2. Which, if any, of the lenses drawn below is:
    (a) a diverging (concave) lens, [1]
    (b) a converging (convex) lens? [1]

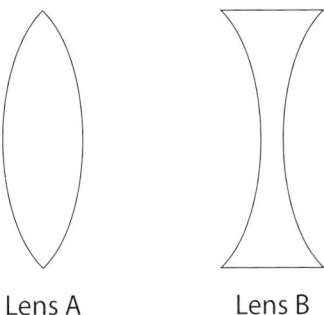

Lens A   Lens B

2.2B DISPERSION AND LENSES

3. (a) Define what physicists mean by the focal length of a converging (convex) lens. [2]
   (b) The diagram below shows five rays entering a lens. Copy the diagram and on it:
   (i) Label the optical centre of the lens. [1]
   (ii) Extend the principal axis of the lens and label it. [1]
   (iii) Show the paths of the rays when they leave the glass and enter the air. [1]
   (iv) Label the principal focus of the lens. [1]
   (v) Use arrows on the diagram to show the focal length. [1]

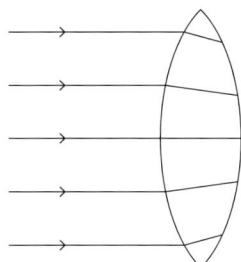

4. A converging lens is used to produce an image that is magnified and virtual. Draw a ray diagram to show how this is achieved. On your diagram mark the principal foci, one on each side of the lens, and the positions of the object and image. Draw also the eye in such a position that it could see the virtual image. [5] *HT ONLY*

5. An object 5 cm tall is placed 6 cm away from a converging lens of focal length 4 cm. On graph paper, draw a full-scale ray diagram to show how the image is formed. Use your ray diagram to find the nature, position and height of the image. [10]

6. By drawing ray diagrams, or otherwise, copy and complete the table below to show the location and properties of the image in a converging (convex) lens. *HT ONLY*

Position of object	Location of image	Properties of the Image			
		Erect or Inverted	Nature	Enlarged or Diminished	Application
Between lens and F	Same side as object, further from lens				
At F	At infinity				Searchlight
Between F and 2F		Inverted	Real	Enlarged	
At 2F		Inverted		Same size	Telescope – erecting lens
Just beyond 2F					Camera
At infinity			Real		Camera

[8] *HT ONLY*

7. The diagram below shows rays of light passing through the front of the eye to form an image on the retina by a person with normal vision.

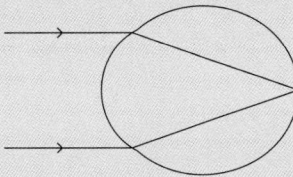

   (a) Draw similar diagrams to show what happens if the person has:
       (i) short sight, [1]
       (ii) long sight. [1]
   (b) Describe the cause of short sight and explain, using a diagram, how the effect can be corrected with a suitable lens. [5]

8. Describe the experiment you would carry out to measure the focal length of a converging lens by the distant object method. [6]

9. Rewrite the following sentences about a data projector, crossing out the incorrect words in each bracket.
   - A (converging / diverging / parallel) lens is used to produce an image of an object on a (film / screen / lens).
   - The image is (real / virtual / neither real nor virtual).
   - The image is (larger than / smaller than / the same size as) the object.
   - Compared to the object, the image is (nearer to / further from / the same distance from) the lens.
   - Compared to the object, we (know / can't tell) that the image is (erect / inverted). [7]

10. The diagram below shows an object in front of the convex lens of a camera. Copy the diagram (you do not need to copy the grey outline of the camera) and on it draw two rays to show how the lens forms the image. On your diagram mark the location of the image and the principal focus of the lens, F.

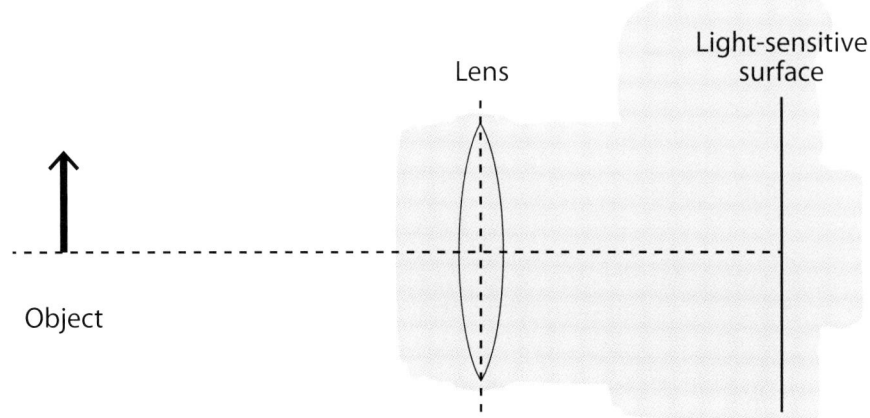

[4]

2.3A Electricity – Simple Circuits and Ohm's Law

1. State the meaning of the nine circuit symbols shown below.

   (a)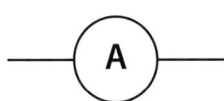

   (b)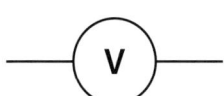

   (c)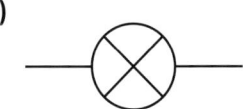

   (d)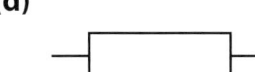

   (e)

   (f)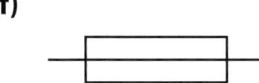

   (g)

   (h)

   (i)

   [9]

2. The diagrams below show batteries made up of individual cells. Each of the cells has a voltage of 1.5 V. For each battery, write down the total voltage between points X and Y.

   (a)

   (b)

   (c)

   (d)

   (e)

   (f)

   [6]

3. (a) State the difference between conductors and insulators in terms of free electrons. [1]
   (b) Copy the circuit diagram below. In the two rectangular boxes draw an arrow to show the direction of conventional current and free electron motion. [2]

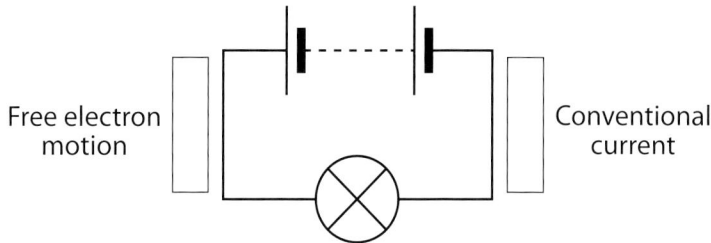

4. A current of 2.5 A flows in a lamp for 5 minutes. How much electrical charge flows in this time? [3]

5. (a) State Ohm's Law. [2]
   (b) Outline an experiment to verify Ohm's Law. [6]

6. The voltage across a length of wire is 0.6 V when the current flowing through it is 0.20 A. Calculate:
   (a) the resistance of the wire, [3]
   (b) the voltage across the wire when the current is 0.25 A. [2]

7. (a) Sketch the voltage-current characteristic graph (V-I graph) for a filament lamp, with voltage on the y-axis and current on the x-axis. The graph should have a (0, 0) origin. [3]
   (b) Using this graph, or otherwise, sketch a graph to show how the resistance of the filament changes with current. The graph should have a (0, 0) origin. [2]

8. The diagram below shows an electrical circuit.

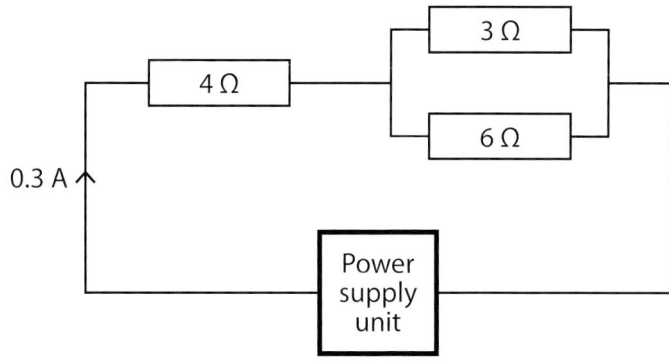

(a) Calculate the voltage across the 4 Ω resistor. [3]
(b) State the current in the 3 Ω and 6 Ω resistors. [2]
(c) Calculate the voltage across the 3 Ω and 6 Ω resistors. [2]
(d) State the voltage of the power supply unit. [1]

9. The diagram shows an electric circuit. Copy and complete the table, by calculating the total resistance between points **A** and **B** for the states of the switches shown in the table.

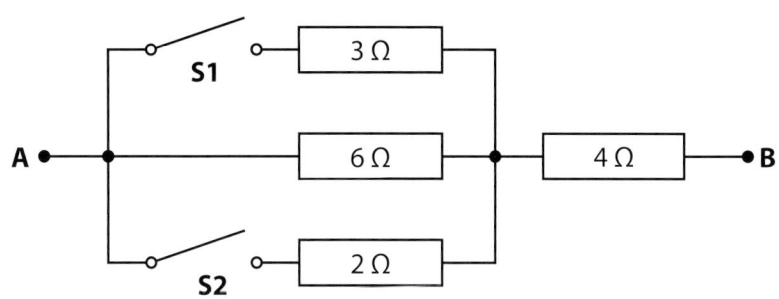

Switch		Resistance between points A and B / Ω
S1	**S2**	
Open	Open	
Open	Closed	
Closed	Open	
Closed	Closed	

[4]

10. A student measures the current in an electrical component for different voltages across it. The student obtains the following results.

Current / mA	0	0.25	0.50	0.75	1.00
Voltage / V	0	2.0	4.0	6.0	8.0

(a) How can you tell, without drawing a graph, that the current in this device is directly proportional to the voltage? [1]
(b) What is the value of the device's electrical resistance? [2]

11. You are provided with a box of resistors, each marked 2 Ω.
Describe how you would connect them together to produce a resistance of:
(a) 1 Ω [1]
(b) 3 Ω [1]
(c) 4 Ω [1]

2.3B Electrical Resistance

1. A student is investigating how the resistance of metal wires change with their length.
   (a) State two properties of the wires which must be the same if the tests are to be fair. [2]

   The student plots a graph of resistance against length.
   (b) Which one of the graphs (**A**, **B** or **C**) shown below is the student most likely to obtain? [1]

   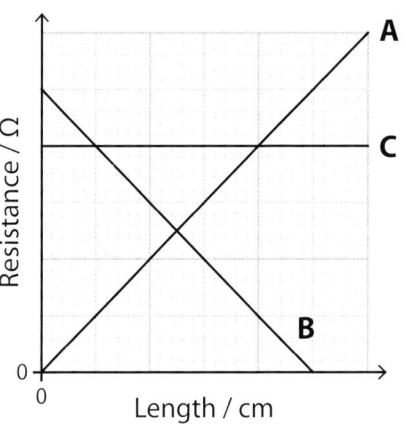

   (c) What conclusion can the student draw from this graph? [1]

2. A student measures the resistance of 90 cm of wire cut from a reel and finds it to be 1.8 Ω.
   (a) What length of wire should be cut from the same reel if a resistance of 2.0 Ω is required? [2]
   (b) Calculate the resistance of a 40 cm length of the same wire. [2]

3. A student is investigating how the resistance of metal wires change with their cross-section area.
   (a) State three properties of the wires which must be the same if the tests are to be fair. [3]

   The results obtained are shown in the table below.

Resistance, R / Ω	48.0	24.0	16.0	12.0	6.0
Cross-section area, A / mm²	0.5	1.0	1.5	2.0	4.0

   (b) How can the student tell by inspecting the table that the resistance is not directly proportional to the cross-section area? [1]

   The student suspects that the resistance is inversely proportional to the cross-section area.
   (c) What straight line graph should the student plot to confirm their idea? [1]

The student confirms that the relationship between the resistance, R, and the cross-section area, A, is:

$$R = \frac{k}{A} \quad \text{where } k \text{ is a constant.}$$

(d) Use the table to find the value of the constant k and state the units in which it is measured. [4]

(e) Use your answer to part (d) to predict the resistance of a wire of cross-section area 2.4 mm². [1]

4. A student measures the resistance of a wire and finds it to be 4.8 Ω. From another reel of the same material she then cuts a piece which is half the length of the first, but with twice the cross-section area. Calculate the total resistance of these wires when they are joined together in:
   (a) series, [3]
   (b) parallel. [2]

5. You are asked to investigate experimentally how the resistance of a metal conductor at constant temperature depends on the area of cross section.
   (a) Identify the independent, dependent and controlled variables in this investigation. [5]
   (b) Which of these variables are continuous and which one is categoric? [5]
   (c) Describe what you would do to carry out the investigation. [6]
   (d) What graph would you plot to confirm your findings? [2]

6. The resistance of a metal wire generally increases as the wire becomes hotter. Explain why this happens, in terms of the movement of free electrons. [6]

7. A student cuts a 50 cm length from a reel of wire and finds its resistance to be 2.50 Ω and its diameter to be 0.30 mm.
   The student then cuts a 50 cm length of wire from a different reel. This wire is of the same material as the first, but it has a different diameter. The student finds that this 50 cm length has a resistance of 10.00 Ω.
   (a) Calculate the area of cross section of the wire of diameter 0.30 mm. Give your answer in mm². [4]
   (b) Show that the diameter of the wire on the second reel is 0.15 mm. [7]

   Hint: Remember that the resistance of a wire is inversely proportional to its area of cross section, if the material and the length are constant. This means that the product, RA, for each reel is constant.

2.3C Electrical Energy and Power, and Electricity in the Home

1. A manufacturer claims that their 35 W LED light bulb gives out as much light energy as a conventional 150 W bulb.
   (a) A physics student correctly states that this is because the conventional light bulb produces much more _____ energy than the LED. What word is missing from the student's statement? [1]
   (b) Assuming the manufacturer's claim is true, how much more current passes through the conventional light bulb than the LED light bulb when both are connected to a 230 V supply? Give your answer to 1 decimal place. [5]

   Both the LED and the conventional light bulb are then tested. The conventional light bulb 'blows' after 2000 hours, but the LED lasts for 40 000 hours.
   (c) How much more electrical energy is used by the conventional bulb than the LED in 2000 hours? Give your answer in MJ. [4]

2. (a) State what is meant by a kilowatt-hour (kW h). [2]
   (b) If electrical energy cost 17 pence per kW h, how much would it cost to run an immersion heater rated at 2750 W for 24 minutes? Give your answer in pence, to one decimal place. [7]

3. Patrick carries out a survey. He discovers that, on average, the time spent by the various members of his family in the shower are:

Patrick	8 minutes
Philip	7 minutes
Mary	9 minutes
Wilma	6 minutes

   The shower is rated at 3.0 kW and electrical energy costs 17 pence per kW h.
   (a) How much does it cost the family to use the shower in this way in an average week? [8]
   (b) Patrick estimates that every day the family uses over 5 million joules of electrical energy in the shower. Is he right? Justify your answer. [2]

4. The diagram shows the inside of a three-pin plug.

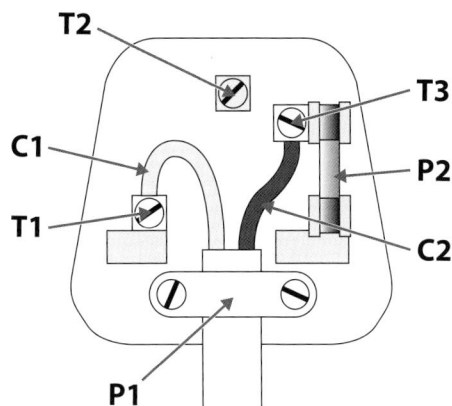

(a) Give the names of the terminals **T1**, **T2** and **T3**. [3]
(b) What colours are the wires labelled **C1** and **C2**? [2]
(c) Name the components labelled **P1** and **P2**. [2]
(d) Describe fully the function of the component labelled **P2**. [4]
(e) Describe fully why no wire is connected to **T2**. [3]

5. The diagram shows a two-way switch.

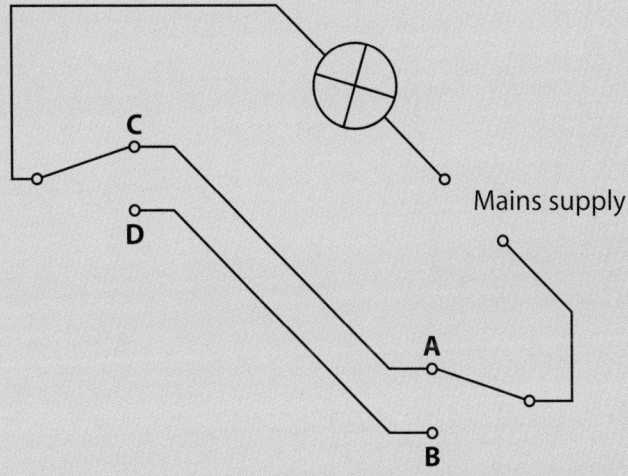

(a) Copy the diagram and mark on it the live and neutral terminals of the mains electrical supply. [2]
(b) Mark on your diagram the position for a fuse, using the correct symbol. [1]
(c) Copy and complete the table below to show the operation of the two-way switch. [4]

Lower switch connected to	Upper switch connected to	Lamp on / off
A	C	
A	D	
B	C	
B	D	

(d) Other than at the top and bottom of a staircase, suggest where such a switch might be used. [1]

UNIT 2: WAVES, LIGHT, ELECTRICITY, MAGNETISM, ELECTROMAGNETISM AND SPACE PHYSICS

6. Some electrical equipment cannot be earthed.
 (a) Explain why this is so. [2]
 (b) What is generally done with such equipment to make it electrically safe? [1]

7. (a) Explain why the plug for most appliances has a fuse. [4]

Appliances with metal cases are usually earthed.
 (b) Explain how the earth wire and fuse together protect the user from electric shock, if a particular type of fault occurs with the appliance. [6]

8. (a) You have the following fuses available:

 1 A
 3 A
 5 A
 10 A
 13 A

Calculate which of these fuses should be used in the plug of:
 (i) an electric kettle, whose rating plate is marked 230 V, 2900 W, [2]
 (ii) an *Xbox One*, whose rating plate is marked 230 V, 112 W. [2]
 (b) Explain why it is:
  (i) foolish to use a fuse with a rating which is much less than that recommended by the manufacturer, and [2]
  (ii) dangerous to use a fuse with a rating which is higher than that recommended by the manufacturer. [1]

2.4 Magnetism and Electromagnetism

1. Draw a diagram to show the shape and direction of the magnetic field around a bar magnet. [2]

2. The diagram shows a cell and a coil wrapped on a cardboard tube.

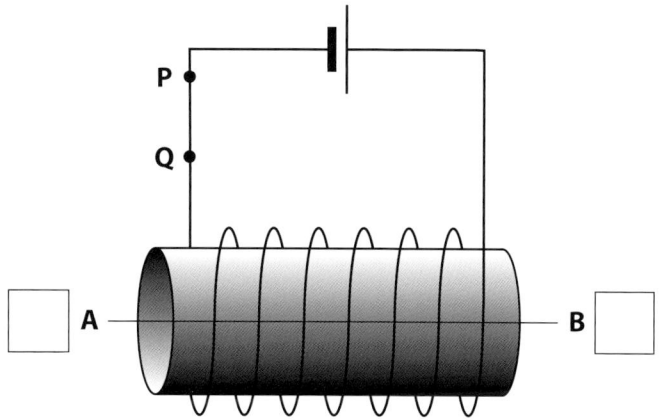

   Copy the diagram.
   (a) Draw an arrow on the diagram to show the current direction between points **P** and **Q**. [1]
   (b) Indicate the polarity of the magnetic field produced by writing the appropriate letters in the two boxes. [2]
   (c) **AB** is a field line along the axis of the coil. Draw an arrow on **AB** to show its direction. [1]
   (d) Draw two other field lines and indicate their direction with arrows. [2]
   (e) State three ways of increasing the strength of the magnetic field inside the coil. [3]
   (f) When an iron rod is placed inside the coil it is called an **electromagnet**.
       In what way is an electromagnet different from an ordinary bar magnet? [2]

3. Describe how you could demonstrate that the strength of an electromagnet is directly proportional to the size of the current in the coil. [6]

4. (a) The diagram shows a wire connected to a cell. The switch is the closed.

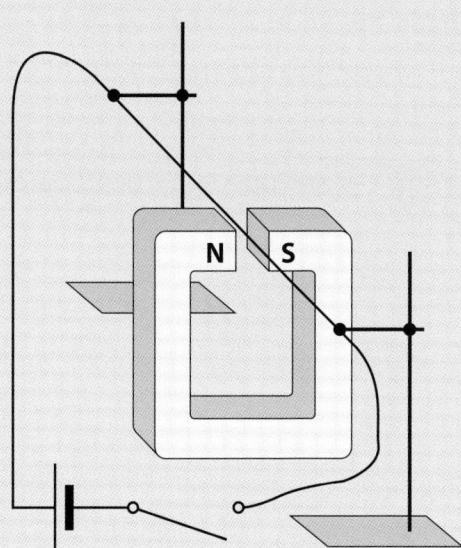

Copy the diagram, and on it mark:
   (i) the direction of the field between the poles of the magnet, [1]
   (ii) the direction of the force on the wire inside the field. Label this force F. [1]
(b) Describe what would be observed if the cell was replaced with an AC source of:
   (i) low frequency (for example, 0.5 Hz), [1]
   (ii) high frequency (for example, 500 Hz), [2]
(c) What equipment used in washing machines uses the effect illustrated by this apparatus? [1]

5. The two diagrams below show a bar magnet and a coil.

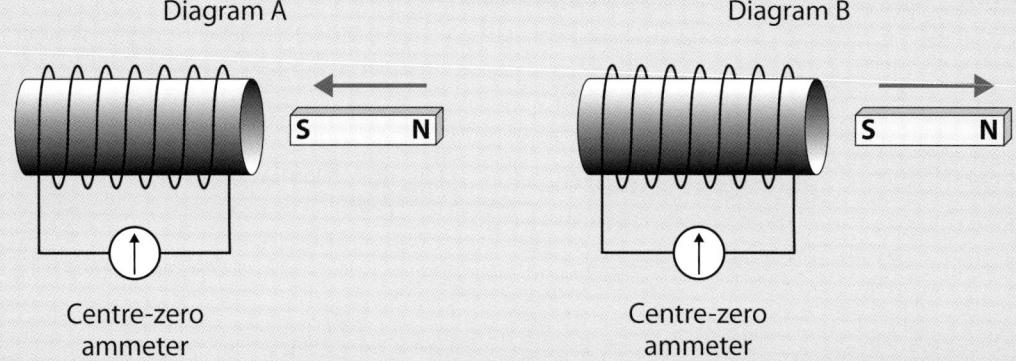

Assume that a current flowing from left to right through the ammeter causes the needle to point to the right of centre.

Describe briefly what is observed on the centre-zero ammeter when:
(a) the south pole of the bar magnet is plunged quickly into the coil (Diagram A), [2]
(b) the magnet is left at rest inside the coil, [1]
(c) the south pole of the bar magnet is pulled quickly out of the coil (Diagram B). [2]

6. (a) What is the difference between AC and DC? [3]
   (b) Three CRO traces are shown below.
       Which of them (**A**, **B** and **C**) are AC and which are DC? [3]

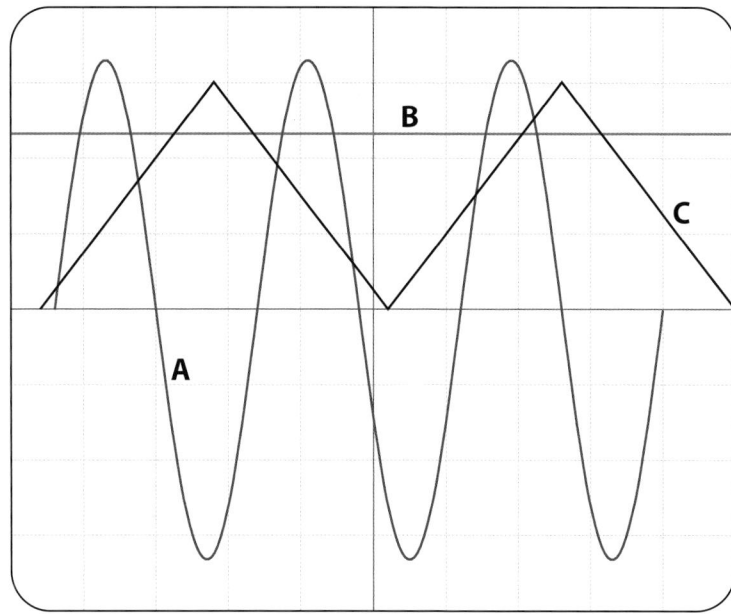

   (c) State a source of AC and a source of DC. [2]

7. The diagram below shows two coils of insulated wire wrapped around a metal core.

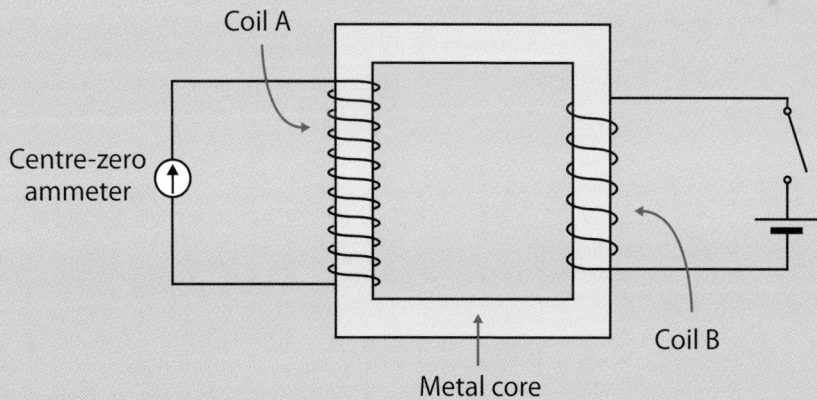

   (a) Describe what is seen on the centre-zero ammeter when the switch is:
       (i) closed, [2]
       (ii) allowed to remain closed and [1]
       (iii) opened again. [2]
   (b) From what metal should the core be made if the effect is to be as large as possible? [1]

   The coils of wire are insulated, so no electric current can flow from the cell through the core.
   (c) Explain, in detail, what is happening when the switch is first closed. [6]

UNIT 2: WAVES, LIGHT, ELECTRICITY, MAGNETISM, ELECTROMAGNETISM AND SPACE PHYSICS

8. The diagram below represents an electricity transmission system.

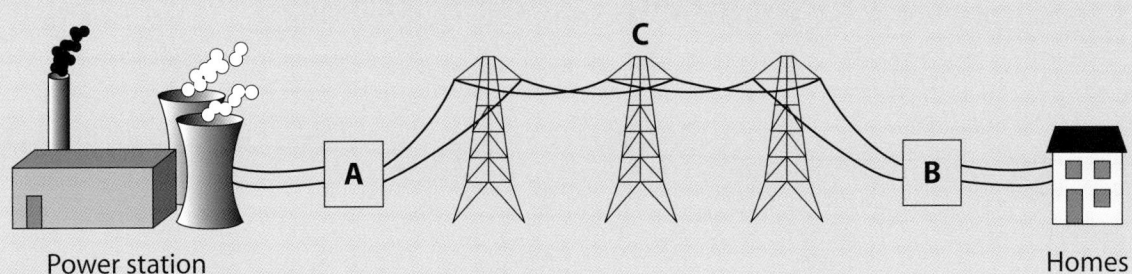

   (a) Name the components labelled **A** and **B**. [2]
   (b) How is the amount of electrical energy lost in the transmission lines kept to a minimum? [3]
   (c) **C** is part of a larger system. What is this larger system called? [1]

HT ONLY

9. (a) Describe the construction of a step-up transformer. [4]
   (b) A transformer has a primary coil of 560 turns which is connected to a 240 V supply. The secondary coil provides an output of 6 V. The current in the secondary coil is 0.4 A.
      (i) Calculate the number of turns in the secondary coil. [4]
      (ii) Calculate the current supplied to the primary coil. [4]

HT ONLY

10. When the input voltage at coil A of a transformer is 24 V, the output at coil B is 6 V. The transformer is now used in reverse.
    Calculate the output voltage at coil A if the input voltage at coil B is 24 V. [3]

2.5A The Earth and Solar System, Stars and the Big Bang Model

1. (a) Name the eight planets of our Solar System, in order, starting with the one closest to the Sun. [2]
   (b) Identify:
   (i) the rocky planet furthest from the Sun, and [1]
   (ii) the gas giant closest to the Sun. [1]
   (c) Name two types of natural heavenly body which orbit the Sun, other than planets. [2]
   (d) What name is given to heavenly bodies which orbit planets? [1]

2. (a) What is the difference between an artificial satellite and a natural satellite? [2]
   (b) State four uses of artificial satellites. [4]

3. (a) What is a stellar nebula? [1]
   (b) Describe how stars come into being. [6]
   (c) What word is required to complete the following sentence?

   Material left over from star formation can be brought together by gravity to form _____. [1]

4. (a) What evidence suggests that stars, including our Sun, are composed mainly of hydrogen and helium? [1]
   (b) Where does most of the helium in our Sun come from? [1]

5. An article in a magazine states: "We are all made of stardust."
Use your knowledge of stars to explain this statement. [2] *HT ONLY*

6. Show the life cycle of a star with a mass similar to that of our Sun by copying and completing the diagram below. *HT ONLY*

Protostar → _____ star → _____ → _____ → _____

[4]

7. Stars which are much more massive than our Sun have a different life cycle than the Sun.
   (a) Copy and complete the diagram below to show their life cycle.

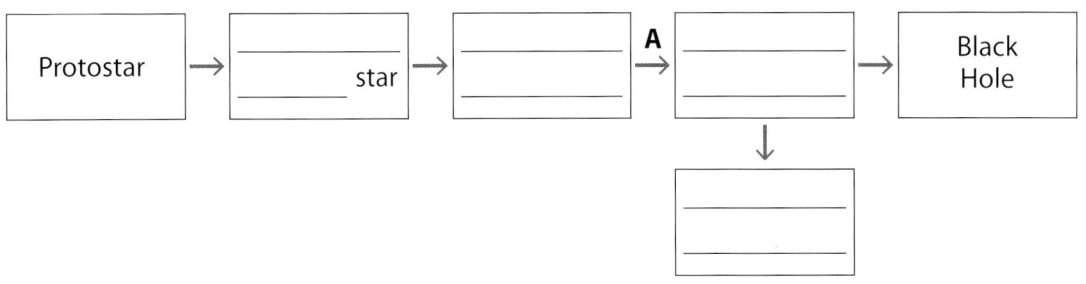

[4]

   (b) Describe what is happening to the star in the change marked **A** on the diagram above. [4]
   (c) Why is the name 'black hole' particularly suitable? [1]

8. (a) At what stage is our Sun in its life cycle? [1]
   (b) What makes our Sun particularly stable in this stage of its life cycle? [1]

9. Most physicists today accept a particular theory as the best one to describe what happened when the universe came into existence.
   (a) What is the name of this theory? [1]
   (b) According to this theory the universe began many years ago. How many years ago? [1]

10. Describe the currently accepted model for the formation of the universe, from its start to the creation of hydrogen atoms. [5]

2.5B Red Shift, CMBR, Space Travel and Life on Other Planets

1. **(a)** What is red shift? [1]
   (b) What does red shift tell us about our universe? [1]

   The diagrams below show the absorption spectrum of light from our own galaxy and light from a neighbouring galaxy called Andromeda.

   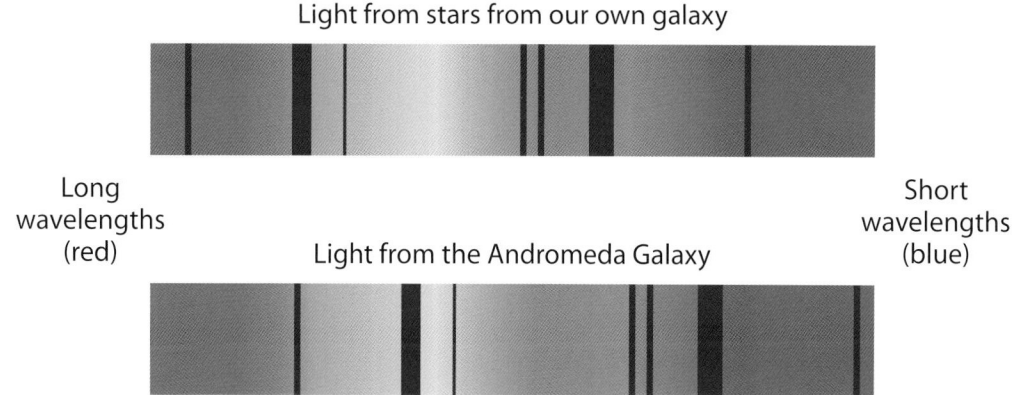

   (c) What can you infer from these spectra about the motion of Andromeda relative to our own galaxy? [1]

2. **(a)** What do the letters CMBR stand for in the context of astrophysics? [1] HT ONLY
   (b) What is the origin of CMBR? [1] HT ONLY

   CMBR was discovered by two American physicists called Penzias and Wilson. HT ONLY
   (c) Why is CMBR important? [1] HT ONLY

3. **(a)** What are exoplanets? [1]

   More and more exoplanets are being discovered every year. One method of doing this is by observing the transit of planets as they orbit their star.
   (b) (i) Why can we see the star, but not the exoplanet? [2]
   (ii) Outline how we can infer the existence of the exoplanet. [3]

4. **(a)** How can the composition of planetary atmospheres be determined? [1]
   (b) Why is the search for oxygen in planetary atmospheres carried out? [1]

UNIT 2: WAVES, LIGHT, ELECTRICITY, MAGNETISM, ELECTROMAGNETISM AND SPACE PHYSICS

5. Give three reasons why, up to the moment, there has been no manned exploration of space beyond the Solar System. [3]

6. (a) What is a light year? [1]
(b) Why is the light year used to measure the distance between Earth and the stars? [1]

HT ONLY

7. The nearest exoplanet is Proxima b, found in the habitable zone of the star Alpha Centauri in 2016. Proxima b is 4.2 light years away from Earth.
(a) Suggest what is meant by the 'habitable zone' of a star. [3]
(b) Light travels at a speed of 3×10^8 m/s. Show that the distance between Earth and Proxima b is approximately 4.0×10^{13} km. You should assume there are 3.2×10^7 seconds in one year. [4]